ABOVE: *In a class that numbered 4,825 vehicles, London Transport's RT 965 was an early post-war member with a distinctive Weymann body and roof route-number box. It is at Hemel Hempstead bus station on a local route in the mid 1950s.*

COVER: *A London General Omnibus Company 'K' type bus built in 1920. This bus belongs to the London Transport Museum and was photographed outside Ye Olde Windmill Inn on Clapham Common, London.*

OLD BUSES

David Kaye

Shire Publications Ltd

CONTENTS

*Published in 1997 by Shire Publications Ltd,
Cromwell House, Church Street, Princes Ris-
borough, Buckinghamshire HP27 9AA, UK.
Copyright © 1982 by David Kaye. First pub-
lished 1982, reprinted 1986, 1992 and 1997.
Shire Album 94. ISBN 0 85263 613 X.*

Printed in Great Britain by CIT Printing Services, Press Buildings, Merlins Bridge, Haverfordwest,
Pembrokeshire SA61 1XF.

ACKNOWLEDGEMENTS
I should like to thank all those who have helped to make this Album possible, and especially D. W. K. Jones,
whose help in providing illustrations has been invaluable. The assistance and advice of Oliver Green, when
he was curator of the London Transport Museum, is acknowledged with gratitude.
Photographs are acknowledged as follows: Barton Transport Ltd, page 12 (top); Clive Birch, page 20 (top);
H. Brearley, pages 5 (both), 6, 7 (lower two), 13 (top), 14 (top); Brush, Loughborough, page 18 (top); Chalk
Pits Museum, Amberley, page 19; City of Liverpool Library, page 7 (top); Reg Davies, page 28; D. W. K.
Jones, pages 10 (top), 14 (bottom), 16, 17 (both), 18 (centre), 20 (centre), 21, 25, 27 (lower two); David
Kaye, pages 1, 22 (top), 24 (top), 27 (top); Lancaster City Council Transport Department, page 15 (bottom);
London Transport Executive, pages 8 (both), 9, 10 (bottom); London Transport Museum, cover, page 4; W.
H. Montgomery, page 22 (centre); National Motor Museum, Beaulieu, page 20 (bottom); J. Nickels, pages
12 (bottom), 13 (bottom); Science Museum, London, Crown Copyright, page 3; Scottish Motor Traction,
page 13 (centre); R. H. G. Simpson, page 24 (bottom); H. J. Snook, pages 15 (top), 22 (bottom); Surfleet
Transport Collection, pages 11 (bottom), 24 (centre); W. Thornycroft, page 18 (bottom).

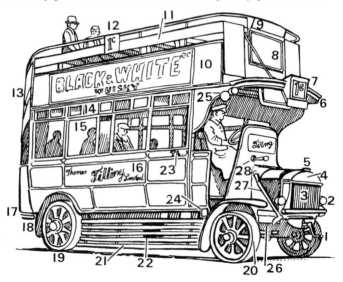

*Diagram of a 1923 double-decker (front offside view). Key to numbered parts: 1 starting handle; 2
headlamp; 3 radiator grille; 4 chassis manufacturer's nameplate (sometimes operator's name substituted); 5 radiator filler cap; 6 driver's canopy; 7 route number plate in slot; 8 via destination board in slot;
9 final destination board in slot; 10 advertisement panel (formerly 'decency board'); 11 guard rails; 12
route number plate in slot; 13 staircase; 14 lower saloon ventilation windows; 15 lower saloon windows
(non-opening); 16 fleet legend on lower panels; 17 platform; 18 mudguard; 19 wooden-spoked wheel; 20
solid rubber tyre; 21 five-bar life guard; 22 petrol tank (under chassis); 23 running number on stencil; 24
driver's foot step; 25 driving mirror; 26 front dumb iron (chassis end); 27 steering column; 28 horn.*

This model of George Shillibeer's original three-horse omnibus of 1829 can be seen in the Science Museum, London. To celebrate the centenary of Shillibeer's vehicle a full-size replica was constructed, and this is on display at the London Transport Museum.

THE HORSE ERA

Long before the first omnibus appeared in Britain, a Frenchman, Blaise Pascal, had operated a bus service in Paris in 1662 using 8-seater vehicles known locally as *carrosses à cinq sous*. The word 'omnibus' seems to have been first used by another Frenchman, M Baudry of Nantes, in 1819 and it was introduced to the British public by George Shillibeer, when he returned from France to start a stage carriage service between the Yorkshire Stingo public house at Paddington and the Bank on 4th July 1829. Short stage services had operated in London from the late eighteenth century but Shillibeer's vehicles justified their name of 'omnibus' (literally 'for all' in Latin) since passengers paid their fares to a conductor on board and could join the vehicle along the route. The complete journey cost one shilling (5p), with a fare for intermediate sections of sixpence (2½p), and Shillibeer's original 22-seat single-deckers were pulled by three horses abreast. Five years earlier John Greenwood had started a service between Market

Street, Manchester, and Pendleton, using 12-seater coaches. Oddly, about the time Shillibeer decided to change to two-horse vehicles, Greenwood switched to three-horse buses!

The 1832 Stage Carriage Act legalised the picking up of passengers anywhere in the street and the number of omnibus operators greatly increased. On 22nd April 1833 Walter Hancock of Stratford in east London started to run his 12-seat steam carriage *The Enterprise* in competition with Shillibeer between the Bank of England and Paddington, but it had to be withdrawn from service after only a fortnight because of technical faults. Soon Hancock placed on the route a second such vehicle, *Autopsy*, which had been tried out between Finsbury and Pentonville. Two larger steamers, *Era* (18-seater) and *Automaton* (22-seater), were in service by 1836. Nevertheless these were not the first steam buses to run in Britain, for Hancock's great rival, Goldsworthy Gurney, had started a service between Cheltenham

3

Three of Walter Hancock's steam coaches: 'Autopsy' (left), 'Era' (centre) and 'Automaton' (right). There was a general fear by the public that their boilers might explode, but although such a fatal accident did occur in Glasgow Hancock's vehicles did not suffer any such mishap.

and Gloucester in February 1831. Four times a day a steam drag pulled a trailer over this 9 mile (14 km) route. In 1833 Maudslay and Field placed a similar vehicle on their London to Greenwich route and John Scott Russell began to run steam buses of his own design on the same route, before trying out one of his 26-seaters between Glasgow and Paisley (7 miles, 11 km).

Meanwhile the 'railway mania' was gathering momentum, and extra buses were needed to serve the new railway stations. Since the mid 1840s some braver passengers had ventured to sit on the roof of single-decked vehicles that were full inside. By the early 1850s special seats were provided for them in the form of a long two-sided bench along the centre of the roof, so that passengers on the top deck sat back - to - back facing out (the opposite to those downstairs, who sat in two rows facing one another). This version became known as the *knifeboard*. It increased the seating capacity to 26. In 1881 the London Road Car Company introduced the first *garden seat* double-decker, in which the seats were arranged in pairs facing forward

on the top deck. By that date 'decency boards' had been fitted, preventing males from obtaining glimpses of the ankles of young ladies, who were now riding on the top deck, and providing a barrier to stop passengers sliding off on to the road, should the bus jerk or brake suddenly. As these decency boards became larger, advertisements began to be placed on them. In addition waterproof aprons began to be provided as protection against rain for those seated on top, whilst straw on the floor acted as a receptacle for spittle and as an insulation against the cold.

In August 1860 an American, George Francis Train, began to operate 20-seater horse trams at Birkenhead, and later he ran similar single-deckers in London. After the passing of the 1870 Tramways Act horse trams gradually spread throughout Britain, until by the end of Victoria's reign most large towns had their own system. Although the steam tram was favoured during the 1880s in some places, horse traction prevailed on most systems. Nonetheless horse buses continued to be used in London and other cities as well as in outlying districts.

4

ABOVE: *T. Howe's one-horse single-decked bus sat 30 passengers. It was used on a route between Gateshead and Newcastle upon Tyne via the High Level Bridge until as late as 1931.*

BELOW: *This 'knifeboard' two-horse double-decker belonging to Nottingham and District Tramways Company was typical of those in use in 1878. As with most other vehicles of this period, the diameter of the rear wheels is much greater than that of the front pair.*

From the 1880s onwards the so-called 'garden-seat' horse bus became popular, enabling passengers on the top deck to see where they were going, as with this example operated by the South Shields Tramways and Carriage Company.

The earlier experiments in steam traction had almost been forgotten and development of mechanically propelled buses was held up by the passing of the Locomotive Act of 1865, the notorious 'red flag' law.

The next group of steam buses appeared in 1897, when the Lifu *Pioneer* ran in London for a short while, before it was sold to the Mansfield Motor Car Company. A second Lifu worked in Edinburgh between 1898 and 1901, whilst others were operating in east Kent. Based on a lorry chassis, the Gillett steam bus of 1899 was tried experimentally as a 24-seater by the Motor Omnibus Syndicate in the London area, whilst in 1902, also in London, another steam vehicle was tried, a Thornycroft, which carried 36 passengers. All these buses were notable for their tall chimneys that pierced the canopy that covered the upper deck.

Other mechanical vehicles were being tried out at the same time. In January 1889 the Ward Electrical Car Company was granted permission by the Metropolitan Police to carry out experimental runs with an electric battery vehicle. In 1891 Mr W. C. Bersey began to use an electric battery double-decker seating 26 passengers between Victoria and Charing Cross. Another such experimental service was operated in Liverpool three years later by the Electric Motive Power Company. In 1896 the Locomotives on the Highway Act did away with the requirement for a man with a red flag and thus encouraged engineers to develop steam, electric and petrol buses.

Amongst the first petrol-engined vehicles were motorised wagonettes, retaining the bodywork of their horse-drawn contemporaries. Both Daimler and Albion were early in this field. In 1898 Thomas Barton of Chilwell, near Nottingham, operated the first motor wagonette excursion, from Mablethorpe, but he transferred the enterprise to Weston-super-Mare for ensuing seasons. This was the era of the char-a-banc, with its rows of bench seats facing forward, fixed to a sloping floor so that each row had a good view over the large hats of the ladies in front of them.

RIGHT: *Although based at Gray's Inn Road, London, the Electric Motive Power Company converted this horse bus to electric battery working in 1894 and used it in Liverpool. Note the exceedingly long steering column, controlled by the driver sitting in the same position as he would if he were coping with the reins of a horse.*

LEFT: *This Thornycroft steam bus was placed into service by the London Road Car Company in 1902 on its Oxford Circus to Hammersmith route. Steel tyres were fitted to its wooden wheels. It gained the nickname 'Twopenny Lodging House' and was later exported to Port Elizabeth, South Africa.*

RIGHT: *In January 1899 the Motor Omnibus Syndicate placed this Gillett steam bus into experimental service. It was based on a lorry chassis (hence the almost equal-size wheels), carrying a modified horse-bus body. It sat only 24 passengers.*

ABOVE: *Amongst the imported buses in use during Edwardian times in London was this De Dion-Bouton from France, belonging to the London General Omnibus Company, which eventually ran 181 of this type. It found favour also with Birch Brothers and with the London Motor Omnibus Company.*
BELOW: *Less than a hundred buses built by the Wolseley Tool and Motor Car Company were sold to London operators. Compared with other early motorbuses the Wolseley 'H' model had a short bonnet. The final drive from its 30 brake horsepower (22 kW) engine was by means of roller chains.*

In January 1908 two Kent firms, J. and E. Hall (Dartford) and W. A. Stevens (Maidstone), pooled their knowledge to produce the Hallford-Stevens petrol-electric chassis. This vehicle was operated by the long established omnibus proprietor Thomas Tilling.

THE EDWARDIAN PERIOD

In November 1907 the following appeared in a Brighton newspaper: 'The bus companies have put upon the road huge machines which have polluted the atmosphere with asphyxiating odours, filled the air with insanitary particles, created so much vibration that the premises have appeared to be experiencing perpetual earth tremors, made such an irritating whirling noise that tradesmen have had to shut their doors in order to hear customers speak, driven carriage people clean out of the street, and freely bespattered with foul oily mud those pedestrians who have braved the terrors of the pavements.'

So the early motorbuses aroused strong opposition, but by 1898 'motor cars' were acting as public service vehicles between Torquay and Paignton; by the end of that year the Honourable C. S. Rolls was trying out an imported 12 horsepower (8.9 kW) Canstatt-Daimler single-decker bus; that summer F. E. Barton had run a motorbus

service at Blackpool; and Dr E. M. Hailey and Mr W. Carlisle MP had begun such a route between Newport Pagnell and Olney using a Daimler. Londoners had their first opportunity of riding on this new form of public transport on 9th October 1899, when a German-built Daimler double-decker running on steel tyres was put into service by the Motor Traction Company between Kensington and Victoria. However, perhaps the most significant date was 26th November 1902, when the London Motor Omnibus Syndicate placed into service some 12-seater Scott-Stirlings on their Marble Arch to Cricklewood route. Two years later Thomas Tilling bought their first motorbus, a 24 horsepower (17.9 kW) Milnes-Daimler registered A6934. Birch Brothers followed suit, and next spring buses of this type were introduced by the London Motor Omnibus Company, and two months later by the large London General Omnibus Company.

Southampton Corporation became the first municipality to operate a motorbus route when from 5th August until 20th December 1901 they ran *hired* vehicles between the Clock Tower and Northam. Then on 12th April 1903 Eastbourne Corporation became the world's first local authority to *own* the motorbuses they ran. The highly successful Milnes-Daimlers were chosen for the route from the Railway Station to Meads. The Great Western Railway became the first railway company to use buses, when they inaugurated a service between Helston and The Lizard on 17th August 1903.

Many of the buses favoured by the London operators were of foreign manufacture. Amongst the most popular were the De Dion-Bouton, the Dürkopp and the Scheibler. Others were of combined British and foreign construction, as was the Straker-Squire-Büssing. In a few instances a British company would buy parts from many places and assemble its own

LEFT: *To compete with the petrol-engined bus, Clarkson of Chelmsford built a much improved steam bus and formed the National Steam Car Company to operate it. The vehicle shown worked the route from Peckham Rye to Shepherds Bush.*
BELOW: *The first of a new generation of electric battery buses was LC5768, built and operated by the London Electrobus Company. In the autumn of 1908 its T. H. Lewis body was given a temporary canopy, but the Metropolitan Police claimed that it was top-heavy, and so it had to be removed.*

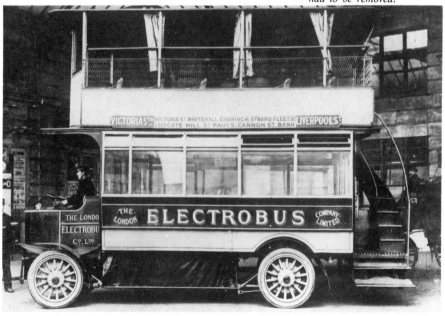

ABOVE: *MN 68 was a 35 horsepower (26 kW) Argus char-a-banc belonging to the Manx Electric Railway Company, which used it on tours on the Isle of Man. It retained the raised seating plan of the horse version of this kind of conveyance. It is seen here at The Bungalow on the slopes of Snaefell.*
BELOW: *There is a raised seating arrangement on this early Daimler char-a-banc operated by Sussex Tourist Coaches for one of the first extended tours from Worthing and Brighton to the Lake District. However, for such prestige work superior bodywork was necessary.*

version of motorbus. An example was the Moss and Woodd 'Orion' with its Swiss chassis, and the Motor Omnibus Construction Company, a subsidiary of the Vanguard group of London operators, established a factory for assembling the parts at Walthamstow. Most of the early motorbuses were chain-driven and had chassis that stood nearly 28 inches (700 mm) from the road surface, so that they needed to have lifeguard struts fitted to their sides to stop exploring children and others from being trapped beneath them. These first motorbuses were called 'normal control' because the driver sat behind the engine (as in a normal car), although in practice with the very first vehicles he was seated on top of the massive, under-powered engine. Local police regulations often limited buses to a maximum speed of only 12 miles per

TOP: *In 1963 Barton Transport built this replica of W963, their very first vehicle, which had carried people to the 1908 Goose Fair in Nottingham. However, whereas that original char-a-banc had been on a Durham-Churchill chassis, this reconstruction is based on a Daimler CB chassis.*

ABOVE: *Just before the First World War a new style of char-a-banc body was introduced, called the 'torpedo'. This example is fitted to a Leyland 'S' chassis and is seen in the livery of Brooke Brothers at Rhyl in 1914.*

hour (19 km/h). Until after the First World War the motorbus body was almost identical with that fitted to horse-bus chassis. Indeed in a few cases the driver even sat where his horse-drawn counterpart sat, steering the bus with a very long column!

The steam bus was also being improved during the reign of Edward VII. In 1903 the Torquay and District Motor Omnibus Company purchased their first steamer from Clarkson of Chelmsford, and these were followed by similar small single-deckers for Eastbourne Corporation, the Great Western Railway and the Sussex Motor Road Car Company. But in 1905 a double-decker version was put on the market and both the London Road Car Company and the London General Omnibus Company bought them. Because they had to carry water tanks containing up to 40 gallons (180 litres) their total weight was nearly $4\frac{3}{4}$ tons (4826 kg), well beyond the Metropolitan Police regulation of $3\frac{1}{2}$ tons (3556 kg), laid down in 1909.

A rival to the Clarkson appeared in 1907 — the Darracq-Serpollet from France.

Great Western Railway number 156 was a Dennis 20 horsepower (15 kW), used largely on feeder routes to stations in 1911. It sat only thirteen, but if the need arose a further three could be accommodated on fold-up seats.

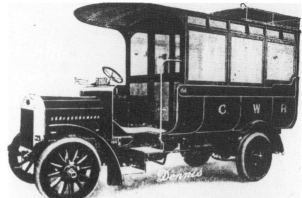

Scottish Motor Traction, like other operators in the First World War, tried to save petrol by converting some of their vehicles to run on coal gas. As in the case of Lothian single-decker number 75, this was stored in a large bag fixed to the roof of the vehicle.

Brooke Brothers of Rhyl ran White Rose Motor Buses, using early Leyland double-deckers. DM 719 was of the 'S4' model of 1912, which had a 45 brake horsepower (33 kW) engine. Refinements included skew gears to keep down noise levels and a water-cooled foot brake.

Leon Serpollet had invented a flash-type generator/boiler in which steam was produced as it was needed. This eliminated the possibility of explosions, while at the same time allowing high pressure. Each double-decker was reckoned to use up 28 gallons (127 litres) of paraffin per day heating the water in its boiler. By 1912 the Metropolitan Steam Omnibus Company was using one hundred of these vehicles, one of which was used to start an express service from London to Maidstone. A. H. Creeth and Sons of Nettlestone in the Isle of Wight used a char-a-banc version.

The Edwardian period was the heyday of the electric battery bus. Although the London Electrobus Company did not fulfil its promise made in April 1906 to have three hundred electric buses running in London, it did at its peak have twenty-one operating. The weight of the forty-four-cell Oppermann batteries amounted to 23 hundredweights (1168 kg), and this slowed them down. In some ways they were in advance of their time, having a final drive in the form of a bevel gear at the end of a propeller shaft to a live axle, instead of the almost universal chain drive. Their appearance in London was short-lived, and in 1909 many of them departed to the depot of the Brighton, Hove and Preston United Omnibus Company, which had already purchased three new Electrobuses. There were also two experimental electric battery buses evolved by Cromptons, but with an unladen weight of 6 tons 7

LEFT: *One survivor from the British bus manufacturers of Edward VII's reign was Straker Squire. Their double-deckers appeared in many fleets as far apart as Douglas (Isle of Man) and Brighton. This vehicle was employed by Ortona on a local Cambridge route.*

BELOW: *In June 1911 the prototype Tilling-Stevens TTA1 petrol-electric bus entered service on Tilling's route from Oxford Circus to Sidcup. It was a quarter of a century before the last TS6s and TS15s were withdrawn from service. An early user was Douglas Corporation, with this TTA1 model.*

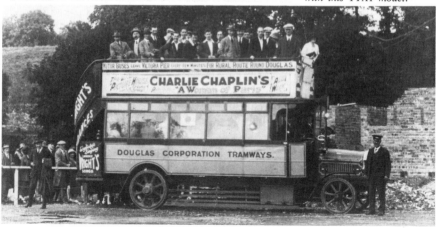

14

ABOVE: *Some of the early single-deckers had open rear platforms, giving them a continental look. Such was P7226, a Leyland, used by the East Surrey Traction Company on its Redhill to Reigate route.*

BELOW: *In December 1916 Lancaster Corporation took delivery of a pair of Edison electric battery single-deckers with 22-seat bodies built by Brush of Loughborough. Here Number 1 recharges its batteries before taking munitions workers out to the Caton Road Projectile Factory.*

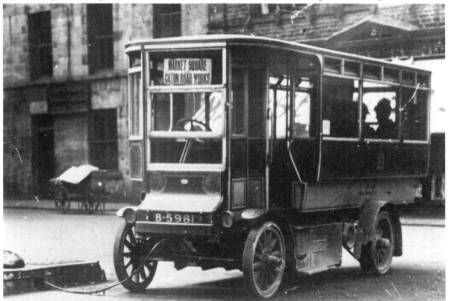

An interesting comparison between the pre-First World War London General Omnibus Company 'B' class seating 34 passengers and the post-war 'K' class, which sat 46. This photograph was taken when they were both stored at Reigate, but now they can be seen at the London Transport Museum.

hundredweights (6452 kg) they failed to meet police requirements.

In towns and cities the bus met competition from the improved electric tramcar. Although the first such systems were holiday novelties at Brighton (Volks, 1883) and the Giant's Causeway, in September 1885 more serious electric tramways opened at Blackpool and between Bessbrook and Newry in Northern Ireland. Starting with Bristol and Coventry in 1895, the electric tramcar soon spread to most large towns in Britain. Then, on 24th June 1911, a new competitor to the motorbus made its debut simultaneously in Bradford and Leeds — the trolleybus. Partly to combat this competition, some ingenious engineers devised the petrol-electric bus. In this hybrid vehicle the motive power came from a petrol engine which drove an electric motor, which gave transmission by an electric clutch and a cardan shaft to the rear axle. The London horse-bus and motorbus pioneers Thomas Tilling took

this up with their successful Tilling-Stevens TTA1. W. A. Stevens also worked closely with J. and E. Hall of Dartford to produce the Hallford-Stevens petrol-electric bus in 1908.

The motorised char-a-banc continued to flourish before the First World War broke out. Starting with the first reliable motor coach, the 24 horsepower (17.9 kW) Milnes-Daimler of 1904, and the equally successful Durham-Churchills, up to thirty passengers could be taken on journeys ranging from a short afternoon trip to extended tours like those undertaken in 1911 by three Leyland 35/40 horsepower (26-30 kW) char-a-bancs named *King George*, *Queen Mary* and *Prince Edward*, which made a 625 mile (1000 km) round tour of the Lancashire coast and the Lake District in a week. The old seating arrangement of bench seats was now being superseded by the so-called 'torpedo' body with a central gangway.

16

ABOVE: *After 1918 many ex-servicemen set up their own country bus routes using former War Department vehicles. Walling of Eastergate, West Sussex, purchased an Austin 2/3 tonner and had a new bus body built for it by Strachan and Brown for his service into Bognor.*

BELOW: *Solid rubber tyres were usual in the early 1920s, when small buses like this Vulcan were bought by the West Hill Bus to run in Bexhill, East Sussex.*

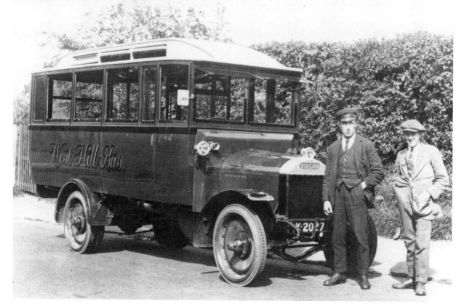

ABOVE: *Southdown Motor Services number 125 is a Leyland 'N' of 1923 with a Short Brothers 51-seat body of 1928. It is preserved at Amberley Museum, West Sussex.*
TOP LEFT: *By 1926 pneumatic tyres were becoming common, especially with single-deckers, like this Guy BA with a 25-seat Brush body, which Leicester City used in 1927 for their new Welford Place to Knighton Lane route.*
CENTRE LEFT: *So-called 'toastracks' came in all shapes and sizes, and this vehicle was an example of the popular runabout built by Guy of Wolverhampton. It was number 2323 in the fleet of Southern National Omnibus Company and is seen here at Weymouth Pier as late as 1938.*
BOTTOM LEFT: *Making its debut at Amberley Museum in 1996 is this replica of Tramcar number 1 (BP9822) of 1924, which ran along Worthing seafront. It is based on a genuine Shelvoke and Drewry 'Freighter' chassis that once belonged to a Truro dust-cart.*

THE PERIOD OF THE PIRATES

When Edward VII came to the throne in 1901 there were only ten motorbuses licensed in London, but 3,736 horse buses. When he died in 1910 there were 1,962 motorbuses to 786 horse buses. Shortly after the First World War began the last of the latter were withdrawn, partly because every available horse was needed for service in France. By 1914 the motorbus construction industry had begun mass-production. When the LMOC ('Vanguard') and LGOC amalgamated, they planned to build large numbers of a specialised bus suitable for London conditions at the LMOC's Walthamstow works. The first of this new 'X' class was completed on 12th August 1909. After X61 had been built, work commenced on an improved 'B' class, which eventually totalled 2,900 vehicles. During the war many of these were requisitioned by the War Department for use as troop carriers, following successful trials in 1908 in the London area.

Both the 'X' and the 'B' had been limited to 34 seats, owing to police requirements, and they were not permitted to have any kind of roof to protect passengers on the upper deck. In body design they still closely resembled the horse bus. Yet in 1910 Daimler had demonstrated its KPL model, an integral-constructed double-decker that had not only an upstairs roof but even an

19

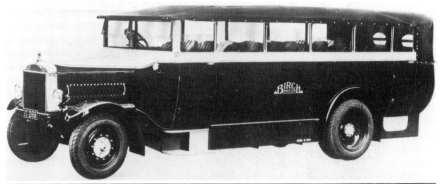

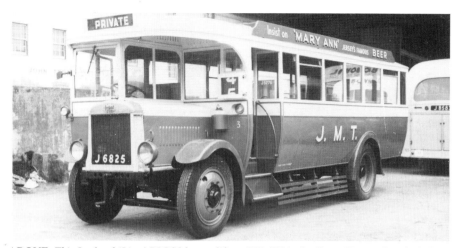

ABOVE: *This Leyland 'Lion' PLSC1 began life as KW 474 in the fleet of Berwick and Blythe. It was shipped to Jersey, re-registered and was still running in St Helier with Jersey Motor Transport in 1956. Subsequently it returned to England and was restored by the Lincolnshire Vintage Vehicle Society as Lincoln City number 1!*

TOP LEFT: *Although originating as early as 1921, this Leyland coach in the livery of Birch Brothers has a much more modern appearance than the contemporary 'torpedo' bodies. It incorporates a favourite feature of the inter-war period, the canvas roof, which could be folded back during hot weather.*

CENTRE LEFT: *Southdown Motor Services number 600 (a Tilling-Stevens B10A2) stands beside their number 818 (a Leyland 'Titan' TD1) in Worthing coach station shortly before the Second World War. Whereas 600 had an all-metal 48-seat body constructed by Shorts, 818 had been fitted with a wood and metal 51-seat body by Brush.*

BOTTOM LEFT: *This 14 seater char-a-banc, built by the American firm Maxwell, was, in 1922, one of the first of many small foreign vehicles purchased by the smaller operators. It incorporates many components from the manufacturer's car series. It was used for club outings before ending up as a working museum exhibit.*

underfloor engine. In Worthing there were 42-seaters operating, and some towns now had covered-top double-deckers. But in 1919, when AEC/LGOC developed their new 'K' type to replace the 'B', although it had a distinctive motorbus-style body, sat 46 passengers and had a more powerful engine, it still ran on solid rubber tyres and had no top-deck covering, even though the *Commercial Motor* had stated in its issue of 13th March 1919 that 'No winter period goes by without the question of the feasibility of improving the London omnibus by covering in the upper deck being revived. This winter the need has been more urgently felt because of the removal of the knee aprons and because of the prevalence of influenza.'

During the war small capacity electric battery single-deckers had been built by Edisons and placed into service at Derby, Lancaster, Southend, South Shields, West Bromwich and York. These vehicles had comparatively short lives and were the last experiments in this form of transport on a large scale until the 1970s.

Many ex-servicemen decided to invest in wartime surplus chassis in 1919. For example, there were spare Austin ambulances and RAF Leylands for sale. Others decided to purchase lightweight chassis like the Model T Ford. In many instances they built their own bus bodies to seat between 14 and 20 passengers. Sometimes this was a removable one to be fitted only for market-day operation; the remainder of the time the chassis bore a flat truck platform or one suitable for transporting farm produce or even coal. Soon the countryside was served by a network of these independently operated rural routes.

At the 1919 Olympia Commercial Motor Show Dunlop displayed its new large 9 inch (229 mm) pneumatic tyres, and

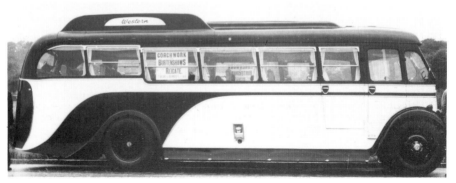

Goodyear 8 inch (203 mm) ones, both suitable for char-a-bancs. But two years passed before vehicles designed to use these began to appear on the market, and then they were foreign makes like Berliet and Laffly-Schneider. Imported small buses and coaches – Chevrolets, Lancias, Reos and Saurers, amongst others – were popular during the 1920s.

By the middle of the decade chassis were being lowered, so that new small models like the Dennis 30 hundredweight (1500 kg) came within 10 inches (260 mm) of the ground in places. These vehicles therefore did not need high steps that impeded the elderly and those with small children. The lower chassis also lowered the centre of gravity of the vehicle and thus helped to convince the police that a covered top could safely be added.

Many privately owned and operated buses and coaches were not affected by the General Strike of May 1926, when the railwaymen came out on strike in support of the miners, and the strike gave a great boost to the new express coach services, which were also benefiting from the tarmacking of main roads. In towns, especially in London, small firms with fewer expenses were competing on the most lucrative routes with long established and larger firms. Not only did they force down fares to uneconomic levels, but they also endangered the safety of both passengers and other road users. There were several cases similar to one which occurred at Arundel in West Sussex, when a one-man operator departed from Littlehampton later than his Southdown Motor Services rival, overtook him, but crashed as a result. Such people were branded as 'pirates', and it was partly due to them that Parliament passed the Transport Act of 1930. This was the principal statute controlling public service vehicles and their use until 1980.

By the 1920s routes were being given numbers (this had happened even earlier in London), rather than each service having its own distinctive livery, which was inconvenient when an operator wished to transfer buses from one route to another. Roller destination blinds at the front of a vehicle began to displace wooden boards, although these were retained for side displays well into the 1930s. In 1930 Tom Barton, the motorcoach pioneer, fitted a Gardner 4L2 diesel engine to his Lancia number 78 and showed that diesels could be safe and economical. Leyland produced the first large modern bus chassis in 1925 when they launched their first 'Lion' with its four-cylinder engine. Two years later the six-cylinder 'Tiger' appeared along with a double-deck version called the 'Titan'. AEC responded with their 'Regal' and 'Regent'. Ministry of Transport length regulations still limited the seating capacity of such vehicles effectively to 32 passengers for a saloon and 56 for a double-decker, although some local authorities (e.g. Eastbourne) had even lower limits. A third, rear-positioned, axle was required on longer vehicles, such as the Leyland 'Titanic' and the AEC 'Renown'.

TOP LEFT: *Lincolnshire Vintage Vehicle Society restored to rally conditions this pair of early Leylands. TF 818 was number 202 in the fleet of Lancashire United Transport and was an LT1 version of the 'Lion'. The double-decker was a TD1 'Titan' and ran as number 53 in the fleet of Bolton Corporation. It has that popular feature of 1929/30, the open staircase leading to an enclosed top deck.*

CENTRE LEFT: *Although the Dennis 'Lancet' Mark I chassis of CZ 7013 dates from 1934, its 31-seat front-entrance body by the local firm of Harkness was fitted to it sixteen years later. Now preserved, it ran for many years as Belfast Corporation number 102.*

BOTTOM LEFT: *Western SMT ran a number of Leyland 'Tiger' coaches with Leyland bodies before 1939. Many were later rebodied as double-deckers, but this one unusually received a rebody by Burtenshaw of Reigate.*

TOP: *Built in 1935, Southdown Motor Services number 1406 was a Leyland 'Tiger' TS7 with a 32-seat body built by the Hove firm of Harrington. It is seen here by Worthing Pier, being passed by a wartime Guy 'Arab' Mark II with a typical so-called 'utility' body.*

CENTRE: *The Dennis 'Ace' was nicknamed the 'Pig' as its protruding engine gave it the appearance of possessing a snout. They were used on lightly trafficked country routes. Between 1936 and 1961 it ran as number 42 in the fleet of Jersey Motor Transport, before its 20-seat Dennis body was converted into a service lorry on Jersey.*

BOTTOM: *In 1930 Gilford introduced their AS6 model, which retained the then rather outdated normal control layout, whilst incorporating more up-to-date features like a floating rear axle. It was powered by an imported Buda six-cylinder engine. This coach has a 20-seat Eaton body, and entered the fleet of Rivers of Ipswich in 1931.*

Birch Brothers sometimes constructed their own bodies for their vehicles. In this case a 25-seater has been built for a Bedford WTB chassis. Number K58 in their fleet, it is seen passing through Highgate village.

REGULATION AND REORGANISATION

In place of a multitude of local authorities deciding which individual vehicles they would license to run within their own boundaries, under the 1930 Transport Act England and Wales were split into ten regions, each of which was controlled by Traffic Commissioners, who decided which operators could work which routes. Normally they decided in favour of those who had provided a good service for the longest time and had previously earned the approval of local councils. This virtually eliminated the pirates of the 1920s. Many of these sold out to the successful applicants, and more and more small firms were bought up during the 1930s. There were already some large operators such as Midland Red (600 vehicles) and Southdown Motor Services (362), and now many of the other subsidiaries of the giant British Electric Traction Company and its chief rival the Tilling and British Automobile Traction Group began acquiring lesser firms within their territory, so that by 1939 Tilling/BAT had over twelve thousand buses and coaches, whilst the BET empire had six thousand. Indeed there were at that date only two truly independent firms of any size left in England and Wales, West Riding Automobile (255) and Lancashire United Transport (223).

The London Passenger Transport Board was established on 1st July 1933, taking over the huge LGOC and its subsidiary London General Country Services, along with London United, Metropolitan Electric, South Metropolitan, the Underground Group and local authority tramways in the London area. Similar amalgamations were taking place in both Scotland and Ireland during this period.

The reduction in the number of operators coincided with the great recession of 1929 to 1932 and resulted in fierce competition amongst the manufacturers of motorbuses and coaches, many of whom were forced out of business. Some that had been particularly favoured by the smaller firms — AJS, Bean, Garner, Halley, Vulcan and W and G — closed, as did some of those that had supplied even the largest operators, including both Gilford and Thornycroft. Gilford had not built their own buses but had assembled them from parts purchased from other manufacturers. Sunbeam and Karrier, amongst others, concentrated on trolleybus orders. Yet, strangely, at a time when the American Chevrolets, GMCs and Reos were disappearing from British roads, another manufacturer from the United States had enormous success within its first few years and is still flourishing in the 1980s. This was Vauxhall Motors' subsidiary Bedford, which in August 1931 sold its first British-made coach to Mr J. Woodham of Melchbourne, Bedfordshire. TM 9547 was the WHB model that sat only 14 passengers, but soon Bedford was turning out the larger WLB and followed this in the late 1930s with the 26-seater WTB, and finally, on the outbreak of war, with the 27- or 29-seater OB.

These were petrol-engined, but the larger fleets were turning increasingly to the diesel engine for their buses. The first production model to incorporate this kind of unit was the Guy 'Arab' in 1933, followed by the AEC 'Regent' 0661, the Leyland 'Titan' TD3, the Leyland 'Tiger' TS4, the Tilling-Stevens D6LA6 (this firm having given up the idea of petrol-electrics), and the SOS DON (designed by Midland Red's Chief Engineer, Mr Shire, hence Shire's Own Specification). Engines were now almost universally mounted in the so-called *forward* control position, i.e. *beside* the driver, apart from a few curious throw-backs like the Dennis 'Ace' (known as the 'Flying Pig'). But some engineers, like Mr G. W. Hayter of Northern General Transport, thought that the power unit could be shifted elsewhere on the chassis, thus providing more room for fare-paying passengers. Therefore he designed the SE6 (six-wheeler) and SE4 with their engines located on the offside of the chassis *behind* the driver. This idea was also taken up by AEC with their 'Q' model, which was much used by London Transport for their Green Line and country bus routes. A similar double-deck version found favour in such places as Aberdeen, Grimsby and Wallasey. London Transport ordered some of the small Leyland 'Cubs' with rear-mounted engines, and later some Leyland 'Tigers' with horizontally mounted engines on the nearside of the front of the vehicle.

For buses operating in flat places like Lytham St Annes, Portsmouth and Worthing, a complicated series of gears for tackling steep hills was unnecessary. Leyland developed what became known as 'Gearless' versions of the 'Lion', the 'Tiger' and the 'Titan'. These vehicles had their model designations suffixed by a small c to denote that they were fitted with a torque converter, which came into action once the engine had built up to 1,200 revolutions per minute and 20 miles per hour (32 km/h). This acted as an infinitely variable gear ratio and thus eliminated the need to change gear (often by double-declutching in those days) every time the bus had to slow down at a stop or at traffic lights and it gave bus travel a smoothness it had hitherto lacked. Doncaster even bought some of the six-wheeled Leyland 'Titanic' TT5c model, although generally the six-wheeler was being phased out by most operators in the late 1930s.

In the years before the Second World War sun bathing became popular, and just as the old open-top motorbus was disappearing from the scene holidaymakers wanted it back! Southdown still had twenty-three 'Titan' TD1s without roofs, but Brighton, Hove and District had to convert some of their older AEC 'Regents' to open-toppers for their summer seafront route. The coaches of the 1920s with folding roofs were now being replaced by newer vehicles with sliding roof panels, and some operators equipped even their double-deckers with these, although they sometimes proved awkward when sudden thunderstorms occurred. Although over one million workers were still unemployed in 1939, the Holidays with Pay Act of 1938 increased the number of people entitled to paid holidays from one and a half million to eleven million. This benefited the bus industry, bringing increased express services, tours and excursions. The growing cinema audiences provided good custom for late-night services.

In 1930 there had been 130 tramway networks still running in Britain. Ten years later, eighty-two of these had closed down. Although in some places, such as Bournemouth, Derby, Hull, Newcastle and Portsmouth, trolleybuses took their place, in many more the new form of transport was the motorbus.

RIGHT: *Portsmouth Corporation number 125 was a Leyland 'Titan' TD4 with a 50-seat English Electric body. From 1935 until 1955 it was in this form, but it was then converted to open-top for the Clarence Pier to Hayling Ferry route.*

BELOW: *The orthodox T469 and the revolutionary Q21 wait in Kingston bus station in 1952. The former was one of the numerous class of AEC 'Regals' which were used by London Transport on both local and Green Line routes. The 'Q' class had fully fronted bodywork, achieved by moving the engine to the offside of the chassis.*

BOTTOM: *Helping out on London Transport's Kings Cross to Norwood route just after the Second World War, when there was a serious shortage of buses in the capital, is this ex-Western SMT Leyland 'Cheetah' LZ2, which had passed into the hands of P. Hearn.*

During both world wars buses and coaches were commandeered by the War Department to transport members of the armed forces. Here, on the Isle of Wight, Southern Vectis numbers 510 (left), a Harrington-bodied Dennis 'Lancet' Mark 1, and 214 (right), a Dodson-bodied AEC 'Reliance', have brought troops out on manoeuvres.

THE SECOND WORLD WAR AND AFTER

During the so-called 'phoney war' of 1939/40 bus production continued on a limited scale, especially of Leyland's new version of the 'Titan', the TD7, which had fully flexible engine mountings. However, when disaster struck first in Norway and then in the Low Countries and France during the spring of 1940, production ceased and the bodyless chassis were declared 'frozen' by the government. By 1942, because of the loss of vehicles due to bombing and the enormous increase in the number of passengers carried, caused by the ban on private motoring, by the coming home on leave of members of the armed forces and by the movement of workers, in certain areas there was a chronic shortage of vehicles. Consequently nearly two hundred TD7 chassis, along with eighty-five Bristol K5Gs and some AEC 'Regents', were sent to specified bodyworks to receive double-deck bodies of a 'utility' design. These had initially only a front destination display, angular rear roofs, and wooden slatted seats. Sometimes they appeared in an overall grey livery, in order to conserve paint supplies. At the same time production of new chassis by Guy Motors of Wolverhampton was permitted.

Since the Ministry of Supply would not release aluminium for bus manufacture, steel had to be substituted, making the new 'Arab' Mark I chassis almost twenty per cent heavier than the pre-war model. These were powered by the rather sluggish Gardner 5LW engine. It became obvious that a six-cylinder 6LW unit was needed, but this was difficult to fit on to a Mark I chassis. So in June 1942 the Ministry of Transport length regulations were amended allowing an extra 9 inches (229 mm) on overall length, to take the Mark II up to 26 feet 9 inches (8.15 m). By 1947 around two thousand Mark IIs had been built. Bedford, from January 1942, was permitted to build a wartime version of its OB, the OWB, of which 3,189 were constructed by September 1945. Most of these carried 32-seat 'utility' bodies. A third source of 'new' buses was to rebody outdated chassis, like the TD1, TD2 and early 'Regents', some of which had been awaiting scrapping when war broke out

As petrol and oil supplies needed to be diverted to the war effort, other ways of cutting the orthodox fuel consumption of buses were tried. Governors were fitted to some engines to prevent them from being run too fast. Whereas during the First World War in some towns gas bags had been carried on the roofs of buses, in this war gas-producer trailers were towed by a few urban-based vehicles. These burnt coke, which gave off a gas that could be used to power the engine.

Express coach services were mostly suspended for the duration of the war, and many coaches were either commandeered for transporting troops or converted into ambulances. The war ended the work of many of the quaint little seafront runabouts of the 1920s and 1930s, such as the Vulcans and Shelvoke and Drewry 'Freighters'. These were sold off as chicken houses, tool sheds and such like.

Wartime technology improved the efficiency of the diesel engine. Although the seven hundred AEC 'Regent' Mark IIs, built between 1945 and 1948, were very much like the pre-war Mark Is, the Mark IIIs had a 9.6 litre engine against the old 7.7 litre one. Similarly the latest 'Titan', the PD1, was still like the former TD7 model, with an improved 7.4 litre engine, but the PD2 version of 1948 onwards was a much more powerful vehicle with a 9.8 litre unit. Likewise the Guy 'Arab' Mark III after 1946 followed the same trend and, indeed, a few were fitted with a 10.35 litre Meadows engine. The same applied to the Crossley DD42s and the Albion 'Venturers'.

Bus operators had to take what vehicles they were given during the war, and some came to like the new types introduced into their fleets, such as the Guy 'Arab' or the Daimler CWA6, and changed their allegiance when free choice came their way again. On the other hand, orders for the single-decker Bedford OWB were rarely followed by ones for the reintroduced OB. Instead, larger companies switched back to the updated Leyland 'Tiger' PS1 model, the AEC 'Regal' Mark II or the Bristol L5G. Between October 1945 and 1950 7,200 Bedford OBs were sold in Britain, but almost exclusively to small coach operators, who wanted a cheap petrol-engined coach in which to carry the passengers so keen for a holiday after six years of war.

The only tramway closed as a direct re-

sult of the war was Coventry, where the famous blitz rendered the system almost beyond repair. For other reasons, trams disappeared from the streets of Huddersfield (1940), Bristol (1941) and Southend-on-Sea (1942). However, in the first five years after the war twenty more tramway networks were closed, as well as parts of the London Transport system such as Barking, East and West Ham and Ilford. The trolleybus, on the other hand, was flourishing, taking over both former tram and bus routes, and new, modern, silent vehicles were being introduced. At the end of 1950 there were still thirty-nine trolleybus systems working in Britain, compared with seventeen tramways. Cardiff (1942) and Glasgow (1949) were the last two places in Britain to convert to trolleybus operation.

1950 marks the dividing line between the pre-war motorbus and its post-war developments. In that year permission was at last given for double-deckers to be 27 feet (8.2 m) long, and single-deckers were increased to a new maximum of 30 feet (9.1 m), without the need in either case for a third axle to be fitted for safety reasons. At the same time the maximum width was increased from 7 feet 6 inches to 8 feet (2.29 m to 2.44 m), and London Transport with its new RTW class of Leyland 'Titan' PD2s was amongst the first to take advantage of these relaxations.

By 1950 the idea of having single-decked buses and coaches powered by horizontally positioned engines situated amidships was becoming a practical reality. Sentinel introduced its SB model in 1948, followed by the four-cylinder STC4 and the more powerful STC6. By 1950 other such models were coming on to the market – the Leyland 'Royal Tiger', the AEC 'Regal' Mark IV and the Bristol LS.

In 1956 London Transport, in co-operation with AEC and Park Royal, introduced the highly successful 'Routemaster' 64-seat double-decker with its air suspension. By 1968 2,760 of this model had taken to the streets, including versions with 72 bus seats (RML), a solitary front-entrance bus (RMF 1254), 57 coach seats (RMC) and 65 coach seats (RCL). Northern General purchased fifty of the front-entrance type. However, a rear-engined version (FRM) tried out in 1967 was regarded as a failure. With the opening of the first stretch of the M1 in 1959 came a new challenge. Fearful of the consequences of a front-tyre blow out, Bedford introduced in 1962 the twin steer VAL with its smaller wheels and three axles. Production of this continued until 1972, but was largely taken up by smaller operators.

In 1954 Leyland brought out their rear-engined 'Atlantean' double-decker, to be followed later by the Daimler 'Fleetline' and in 1966 by the Bristol VR. Likewise rear-engined single-deckers appeared – some a great success such as the Bristol RE, others largely ignored as was the Leyland 'Panther'. There now followed a disappearance from the scene of chassis manufacturers such as AEC, Daimler and Guy, along with bodybuilders of distinction, like Park Royal, Roe and Massey. Into this vacuum returned Dennis Brothers with their 'Dominator' double-decker and

foreign, imported chassis especially from Scania and Volvo, as well as bodies constructed by Caetano and Van Hool.

As passenger numbers and mileage operated continued to fall rapidly throughout the 1960s and 1970s government aid came in the form of a fuel rebate and grants for vehicles designed specifically for stage carriage duties. Local authorities were allowed to give subsidies for non-profitable rural routes. On 20th February 1967 the Post Office launched its first post bus service between Llanidloes and Wye using a Morris J2 7-seater minibus (KVB 103D). By June 1975 there were seventy-six such routes. With the passing of the 1968 Transport Act six Passenger Transport Executives were set up in large conurbations (West Midlands, Greater Manchester, Merseyside, South Yorkshire, Tyne and Wear, and West Yorkshire). In addition the existing BET companies sold out to the new National Bus Company, which was established on 1st January 1969.

RALLIES, RUNS AND RUNNING DAYS

During the 1990s there has been a further considerable expansion in the events that attract thousands of bus enthusiasts.

These basically take three forms. The first is the simple static rally, of which there is now at least one each weekend during the season that starts at the end of March and can last as late as the beginning of December. Venues vary from a disused chalk pit (Amberley, West Sussex) to the former Brooklands race track (Cobham Bus Rally, Surrey). Secondly there are long established runs, such as the London to Brighton (May), the Irish Transport Trust Run from Carrickfergus (April), the Leicester Road Run (August) and the Trans-Pennine Run (August). Thirdly there are the more recently instituted running days, amongst which are

those of King Alfred buses running on their old routes based on Winchester (New Year's Day) and the Delaine Running Day at Bourne, Lincolnshire (August Bank Holiday Saturday). Even Christmas Day is not exempted, when former West Yorkshire Road Car vehicles operate on local routes in Keighley. Details appear each year in the April edition of *Buses*.

There is yet another way to experience old buses and coaches. Some run on excursions, as in Jersey and Callander, using such vehicles as Bedford OBs. Yet another form of interest in past types can be found in the proliferation of models, which now cover vehicles from Edwardian times up to the present, and which are depicted in a great variety of operators' liveries.

FURTHER READING

Barket, T. C., and Robbins, M. *A History of London Transport*. Allen & Unwin, 1963.
Birks, John A. *National Bus Company 1968-1989*. Transport Publishing Company, 1990.
Booth, Gavin. *The British Motor Bus – An Illustrated History*. Ian Allan, 1979.
Booth, Gavin. *The Heyday of the Classic Bus*. Ian Allan, 1994.
Flanagan, Patrick. *Transport in Ireland, 1880-1910*. Transport Research Associates, 1969.
Fletcher, William. *Steam on Common Roads*. David & Charles, reprint 1972.
Hibbs, John. *The History of British Bus Services*. David & Charles, 1968.
Hibbs, John (editor). *The Omnibus*. David & Charles, 1971.
Joyce, T. *Town Transport in Camera*. Ian Allan, 1980.
Kaye, David. *Buses and Trolleybuses before 1919*. Blandford, 1972.
Kaye, David. *Buses and Trolleybuses, 1919-1945*. Blandford, 1970.
Kaye, David. *British Battery Electric Buses*. Oakwood Press, 1976.
Kaye, David. *The British Bus Scene in the 1930s*. Ian Allan, 1981.
Lockwood, Stanley. *Char-a-Bancs and Coaches*. Marshall, Harris & Baldwin, 1980.
Robbins, George. *General Buses of the Twenties*. Image Publishing, 1996.
In addition the PSV Circle and the Omnibus Society have jointly published fleet histories of most of the major bus operators and also a series on smaller operators county by county. Further details from the PSV Circle, 7 Linden Row, Dunstable, Bedfordshire LU5 4NB.

PLACES TO VISIT

An asterisk (*) denotes that only some of the exhibits are listed here.

Amberley Museum, Amberley, Arundel, West Sussex BN18 9TL. Telephone: 01798 831370. Exhibits (*): a replica Southdown country garage with that operator's vehicles including Leyland 'N' 125 (CD 5125), TD1 873 (UF 6473), along with ex-Worthing Motor Services 1914 Tilling-Stevens IB 552 and replica Tramocar 1 (BP 9822).

Aston Manor Transport Museum, 208-216 Witton Lane, Aston, Birmingham B6 6GE. Telephone: 0121-322 2298. Exhibits (*): examples of Midland Red vehicles including C1 coach 3311 (KHA 311), D9 double-decker 5370 (6370 HA) and S21 single-decker 5870 (LHA 870F). Amongst Birmingham City vehicles are Leyland PS2 2231 (JOJ 231) and Daimler CVD6 2707 (JOJ 707). Also on display are Sentinel STC4 GUJ 608, Guy 'Wolf' SB 8155 and Maudslay coach DDM 652.

Birkenhead Transport Museum, Birkenhead Tram Shed, Pacific Road, Birkenhead, Merseyside. Telephone: 0151-666 2656. Exhibits (*) include many local buses, e.g. Wallasey early Leyland 'Atlantean' 1 (FHF 457) and Birkenhead Leyland PD2/40 10 (FBG 910).

British Commercial Vehicle Museum, King Street, Leyland, Lancashire PR5 1LE. Telephone: 01772 451011. Exhibits: 1896 horse bus of Edinburgh and District Tramways; Chocolate Express Omnibus Company Leyland LB5 of 1924; a 1929 14-seater Bean (UL 1771); London Transport RT 1798 (KYY 653); Warrington Corporation Foden PVD6 112 (OED 217); Ribble Leyland 'Tiger Cub' 111 (JRN 29) with a Burlingham 'Seagull' coach body.

City of Portsmouth Preserved Transport Depot, 48-54 Broad Street, Old Portsmouth, Hampshire. Telephone: 01705 376940 or 363478. Exhibits (*): the 1876 'Fawley Flyer' coach; 1919 vintage Thornycroft 'J' 1 (BK 2986); Leyland TD4 open-topper 8 (RV 6368); wartime Bedford OWB 170 (CTP 200); Leyland PD1 189 (DTP 823). Also Southdown Leyland 'Cub' 26 (ECD 526) and Hants and Sussex Bedford OB 31 (EHV 65).

Cobham Bus Museum, Redhill Road, Cobham, Surrey KT11 1EF. Telephone: 01932 864078 (weekends only). Exhibits (*): this museum is devoted to London Transport and its predecessors. The vehicles include Dennis 4-tonner D142 (XX 9591); the sole surviving AEC 'Regent I' with a Tillings open stairs body, ST922 (GJ 2098); AEC 'Q' Q83 (CGJ 188); utility Guy 'Arab II' G351 (HGC 130); AEC 'Regal IV' prototype UMP 227; BEA AEC 'Regal IV' coach MLL 740.

Dover Transport Museum, Old Park, Whitfield, Dover, Kent CT16 2HQ. Telephone : 01304 822409 or 204612. Exhibits (*): there is a concentration on East Kent Road Car vehicles including Leyland-Beadle rebuild coach GFN 273 and a pair of AEC 'Regent V' double-deckers: AFN 780B and GJG 751D (open top). One of the trio of ex-Llandudno Dennis 'G' toastracks (CC 9201) is also housed here.

East Anglia Transport Museum, Chapel Road, Carlton Colville, Lowestoft, Suffolk NR33 8BL. Telephone: 01502 518459. Exhibits: Lowestoft Corporation AEC 'Regent II' 21 (GBJ 192) and AEC 'Swift' 4 (YRT 898H); Eastern Counties Omnibus Company Bristol LL5G number LL108 (KAH 408); all these have locally built Eastern Coachwork bodies. In addition there is the well-known Leyland Lion PLSC KW 1961 and London Transport RTL 1056 (LLU 829).

Glasgow Museum of Transport, Kelvin Hall, 1 Bunhouse Road, Glasgow G3 8DF. Telephone: 0141-287 2720. Exhibits: Albion 'Venturer' B92 (EGA 79) and Leyland 'Atlantean' LA1 (FYS 998).

Ipswich Transport Museum, Old Trolleybus Depot, Cobham Road, Ipswich, Suffolk IP3 9JD. Telephone: 01473

715666. Exhibits (*): Ipswich Corporation's first motorbus AEC 'Regent III' 1 (ADX 1), AEC 'Regal IVs' 9/10 (BPV 9/10) and AEC 'Swift' 82 (JRT 82K). Eastern Counties is represented by Tilling-Stevens B9B 78 (DX 6591), Dennis 'Ace' D973 (CAH 923) and Bristol L5G LL74 (CVF 874). There is also a 1932 vintage Bedford WLB (WV 1209) that was once operated by Foreman of Orford, before becoming the 'Pink Elephant' mobile tea bar!

Keighley Bus Museum, 29 Ethel Street, Keighley, West Yorkshire BD20 6AN. Telephone: 01535 603379. Exhibits (*): many of these are of local origins, e.g Bradford Corporation AEC 'Regent III' 82 (HKW 82); Halifax Corporation Leyland PD2/37 43 (PJX 43); Leeds City AEC 'Regent V' 980 (ENW 980D); West Yorkshire Road Car Company Bristol 'Lodekka' FS6B 1810 (KWT 642D); Yorkshire Woollen District Leyland 'Atlantean' 773 (MUA 870P). However, amongst other vehicles on display are Crosville Motor Services Leyland TD5 M52 (CFM 354) and Rawtenstall Corporation Leyland 'Lion' LT3 61 (TF 6860) dating from 1931.

Lincolnshire Road Transport Museum, Whisby Road, Doddington, Lincoln LN6 0GT. Telephone: 01522 500566 or 689497. Exhibits (*): as well as local Lincoln City Leyland TD7 64 (BFE 419), Leyland 'Lion' LT1 5 (VL 1263) with its rare locally built Applewhite body, and Guy 'Arab III' with local Ruston air-cooled engine 23 (DFE 383), there are several ex-Lincolnshire Road Car buses such as Leyland 'Tiger' TS7 1411 (FW 5696) and Bedford OB (with cut-away near side for Skegness promenade duties) 1004 (LTA 752). Other vehicles include Bolton Corporation's open stairs Leyland TD1 53 (WH 1553), the unique Leyland 'Badger' (KW 7604) that was a Bradford Corporation school bus, and Trent's mobile booking office from Skegness, SOS 'DON' 321 (RC 2721).

London Transport Museum, 39 Wellington Road, Covent Garden, London WC2E 7BB. Telephone: 0171-836 8557. Exhibits on display include AEC/LGOC B340 (LA 9928), AEC K424 (XC 8059), AEC NS1995 (YR 3844), AEC 'Renown' LT165 (GK 5323), AEC 'Regal' T219 (GU 5486), Leyland 'Tiger' FEC TF77 (FJJ 774), the highest RT, 4825 (OLD 589), 'Routemaster' RM 1737 (737 DYE).

Manchester Museum of Transport, Boyle Street, Cheetham, Manchester M8 8UL. Telephone: 0161-205 2122. Exhibits (*) in the main cover operators from the Greater Manchester conurbation and include Manchester Carriage Company's number 2 horse bus, North West Road Car Leyland 'Tiger' TS4 170 (DB 5070), Ribble Motor Services Leyland 'Lion' PLSC1 295 (CK 3825), and Leyland 'Cheetah' 1568 (RN 7824); Bullock of Cheadle's Foden PVSC6 LMA 284; British Aerospace Leyland 'Comet' MUE 990; Beeline Buzz Company's Freight Rover minibus D63 NOF. There are many ex-Manchester City vehicles varying in age from 1930 vintage 28 (VR 5742), a Leyland 'Tiger' TS2, up to 1001 (HVM 901F), a 1968 Leyland 'Atlantean'. The 1975 Seddon Lucas electric battery bus, SELNEC EX62 (GNC 276N) is also on view, as well as buses from the municipal fleets of Ashton-under-Lyne, Bolton, Bury, Leigh, Oldham, Ramsbottom, Rochdale, Salford, Stockport and Wigan.

Nottingham Heritage Centre, Mere Way, Ruddington, Nottingham NG11 6NX. Telephone: 0115-940 5705. Exhibits (*): this is Barton territory and amongst former vehicles of that Chilwell operator are a replica of their number 1 (W 963), Leyland 'Cub' 284 (CRR 819) and the unique lowbridge Dennis 'Loline III' 861 (861 HAL). Other local operators represented include South Notts Leyland 'Lion' LT5 17 (VO 8846) and Leyland 'Royal Tiger' 42 (MAL 310); Trent Leyland 'Tiger Cub' 194 (YRC 194); Nottingham City's first Leyland 'Atlantean' to carry the distinctive Nottingham-style Northern Counties bodywork 523 (STO 523H).

Oxford Bus Museum, Station Yard, Long Hanborough, Oxfordshire. Telephone: 01993 883617. Exhibits (*) include veteran City of Oxford Tramways Company Daimler 'Ys' dating from 1915 (39, DU 4838) and 1917 (45, FC 2602) and later City of Oxford Motor Services vehicles ranging from AEC 'Regent' GA16 (JO 5403) of 1932 to several AEC 'Bridgemasters' and their successors the 'Renowns' and Daimler 'Fleetline' 430 (UFC 430K) of 1971. Other local vehicles include Chiltern Queens' AEC 'Reliances' YNX 478 and 850 ABK. Amongst interesting recent additions is Midland Red 1047 (HA 4087), an SOS 'DDRE' of 1933.

Sandtoft Transport Centre, Belton Road, Sandtoft, near Doncaster DN8 5SX. Telephone: 01724 711391. Exhibits (*): Doncaster Corporation is represented by several vehicles including Leyland 'Royal Tiger Cub' 55 (UDT 455F) and Daimler CVG6LX 206 (KDT 206D). Other Yorkshire operators represented include a pair of Felix Motors' AEC 'Reliances' (YWX 795 and 9629 WU); Kingston-upon-Hull Corporation Leyland 'Atlantean' 217 (JRH 417E); Sheffield City Daimler 'Fleetline' 754 (WWJ 754M); and Yorkshire Pullman AEC 'Regent III' 64 (JDN 668).

Scottish Vintage Bus Museum, Lathalmond, Dunfermline, Fife. Telephone: 01383 720241. Exhibits (*): an opportunity to see a variety of bodywork by Walter Alexander, e.g. Alexander (Midland) Leyland 'Tiger' OPS2 10 (DMS 823); Aberdeen 155 (BRS 37), a Daimler CWA6; Western Scottish Leyland 'Leopard' PSU3 L2629 (OSJ 629R).

Sheffield Bus Museum, Tinsley Tram Sheds, Sheffield Road, Tinsley, Sheffield S9 2FY. Telephone: 0114-255 3010. Exhibits (*): local Sheffield City vehicles including Leyland 'Tiger' PS1 215 (JWB 416), AEC 'Regent III' 2116 (OWE 116); AEC 'Swift' 54 (DWB 54H). Other items include Alexander (Midland) Leyland TD7 (WG 9180); Western National Omnibus Company Bristol 'Lodekka' LD6G 1943 (VDV 760); Grimsby Cleethorpes Transport Daimler CVG6LW 57 (TJV 100); Bristol Omnibus Company Bristol MW6G 2522 (357 MHU).

Ulster Folk and Transport Museum, Cultra, Holywood, Co. Down, Northern Ireland BT18 0EU. Telephone: 01232 428428. Exhibits: Belfast City Transport Dennis 'Lancet' 102 (CZ 7013); Great Northern Railway GNR 324 (ZD 726); Northern Ireland Road Transport Board Bedford OWB GZ 783; Belfast City Daimler Fleetline 2857 (EOI 4857).